1.00

HARLESTON FAIR
The Story of Robert Greene

A Tudor author from Norfolk, who in his play,
Friar Bacon and Friar Bungay shows
Shakespeare how best to use
local knowle

GW00689545

by
Bill & Helen K⌐⌐⌐⌐⌐⌐

The historical background to the play *The Honourable History of Friar Bacon and Friar Bungay* and its author, Robert Greene, especially with regard to the connection with Harleston and other places in the Waveney Valley.

Omne tulit punctum qui miscuit utile dulce
(He has gained every point who has mixed
the useful with the sweet)
Robert Greene's motto, taken from Horace

HARLESTON 2006

Published by ecollectit Ltd., 2006
PO Box 30, Harleston, Norfolk, IP20 9AA

Copyright

© Harleston Players

All rights reserved. No part of this publication may be reproduced, stored in a retrieval system or transmitted, in any form or by any means, electronic, mechanical, photocopying or otherwise without the permission of the publisher, ecollectit Ltd.

The grant for this project is from the Local Heritage Initiative, devised and run by the Countryside Agency. It is a national grant scheme that helps local groups invest in, explain and care for their local landscape, landmarks, tradition and culture. LHI grants are funded by the Heritage Lottery Fund with additional sponsorship from the Nationwide Building Society.

ISBN 0-9549376-7-8

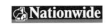

Contents:

Preface

The pioneering literary productions of Robert Greene have languished far too long in the shade of William Shakespeare. By concentrating its attention on the 'Bard of Avon' as the sole instigator of the flowering of the English language, the world has pushed aside the work of a Norfolk author who was part of a group of men who were the essential precursors of Shakespeare in that wonderful explosion of words in the age of Elizabeth I. In neglecting Greene, the literary world has neglected the important contribution of East Anglia to our written heritage.

Greene's most successful comedy, *The Honourable History of Friar Bacon and Friar Bungay*, has not been entirely forgotten by modern actors. The Cambridge University Marlowe Society performed it in July and August 1960 at the Cambridge Arts Theatre, Stratford-upon-Avon Open Air Theatre, and the Lyric Opera House London. Ian McKellen played Lacy, Earl of Lincoln; Derek Jacobi, Edward, Prince of Wales; Trevor Nunn was Miles, and Corin Redgrave King Henry III.

In a further attempt to redress the balance somewhat, Harleston Players are reviving *The Honourable History of Friar Bacon and Friar Bungay*, using a version specially adapted for the occasion by Cathy Gill, but without missing anything of the original themes and language.

Because of the lack of knowledge of Greene and his works by the public, and the rarity of any relevant material, we have gathered together what there is, put it into the context of the time that gave rise to its existence and published it in book form.

The title of the book, *Harleston Fair*, was chosen to emphasise the significance of Harleston and the surrounding areas of Norfolk and Suffolk in the romantic pastoral theme which weaves in and out of the action throughout the play. The use of local knowledge by Greene in constructing this play within a play was an innovation that obviously worked for the customers at the Rose Theatre and we have tried to find out what events of the time might have made Harleston a name which was familiar to Greene and his audience.

1

We do not wish to diminish the parts that other pre-Shakespearean writers played in the so called English Literary Renaissance. Indeed Marlowe, Peele, Lyly, Kyd, and Nashe were all very much involved in its development. They were either friends and collaborators of Greene, or in the case of Lyly, also a source of inspiration.

Thomas Nashe, a particular associate of Greene, can also be claimed for East Anglia, since he was born in Lowestoft where his father was a minister. He wrote his final work, *Lenten Stuffe*, about Yarmouth and its famous product the red herring. He moved to West Harling in Norfolk when he was six as his father had been translated to that parish. He was educated at home and went up to Cambridge in 1581 at the age of fourteen. Although he was nine years younger than Greene, they were contemporaries for two years at Cambridge since Greene did not graduate until 1578, taking his MA in 1583.

In writing the story of Robert Greene and his connection with the market town of Harleston, we feel we have tried to put his position in the field of the history of English literature in proper perspective. We hope, however, that we have not in our enthusiasm for all things Norfolk/Suffolk and Waveney Valley, over exaggerated his importance with respect to his contemporaries and his literary beneficiary, William Shakespeare.

We would like to thank our friends in the Norfolk Heritage Centre in the Forum, Norwich for their unstinted assistance, and also our personal friends for their help and support. We acknowledge the use of quotations from the facsimile reproduction of *The Honorable Historie of Frier Bacon and Frier Bungay,* published by the Scolar Press, and the use of the facsimile of part of Greene's *Groatsworth of Wit* that was reproduced in the book, *In Search of Christopher Marlowe*; a pictorial biography by A.D. Wraight & Virginia F. Stern, published by Adam Hart (Publishers) Ltd., Chichester, in 1993.

1   Elizabethan England

The birth of Robert Greene in 1558 coincided with the rebirth of a more humanist world in England after the brief re-imposition of control from Rome by 'Bloody Mary'. That is not to say that the reign of her half sister Elizabeth, daughter of the Norfolk born Anne Boleyn, was not much less bloody in its efforts to impose a national form of Christianity on her subjects. Rather, she herself, with all her human desires and interests, was in a position to exercise her own power as head of the secular and religious state, independent of all other states and principalities, without the religious fanaticism of her sister. This made her feel responsible to her subjects for her actions and she could not blame outside forces for any problems they might have to suffer. She was dependent on advice from her councillors for the smooth running of the state, particularly Sir William Cecil, her first Secretary of State who became Lord Treasurer in 1572 with the title of Lord Burleigh, and who continued to serve her faithfully until his death in 1598.

Robert Dudley, her favourite, the Earl of Leicester, was also influential but lost much of his power over her after the suspicious death of his wife Amy Robsart in 1560 leading people to believe that it was part of a plot to enable him to marry Elizabeth and possibly to restore friendship with Catholic Spain. Notwithstanding the swings and vicissitudes of Protestant and Catholic struggles for dominance both within the British Isles and the rest of the Christian world, the sole driving force of Elizabeth's rule was survival of herself as queen and the independence of the English nation. This new secular state had become an organism run by humans for humans, bereft of blind medieval religious thought control.

The net effect was a more, what we would call, permissive society. Continuing the work of Edward VI's reign, schools and colleges were re-founded outside the influence of the dissolved monasteries educating a new breed of literate humanists. These were the articulate members of society that Elizabeth and her advisors had to get on side before she could defeat her enemies, and before she could frustrate the papal crusade led by Philip II of Spain who, as joint sovereign with his wife Mary, Elizabeth had replaced on the throne of England.

Robert Greene and the Age of Elizabeth were both thirty years old when the Spanish Armada was defeated and the threat of the re-imposition of control by the Pope in Rome by war and conquest effectively removed.

The driving force behind the revolutionary changes in society during the Tudor period was the printing press, introduced to England by William Caxton in 1477. Tyndale translated the New Testament in 1525 and in the first years of Elizabeth's reign a copy was placed in every parish church. A translation by John Knox was widely read, making fine literature available to the masses and encouraging the spread of literacy. At the same time translations of the Greek and Roman authors were being published in England, together with French, Italian and German literary works. These encouraged the 'New Learning', providing examples of literary styles in poetry and prose, and stories and characters for the new literati to use in their own works.

Both the Old World and the New World, (discovered by the Italian Christopher Columbus in 1492), were in turmoil throughout the sixteenth century. Not only did Henry VIII break the bonds between the church of Rome and the monarchical state, but other kingdoms also began to spread their nationalist wings. So-called religious wars were fought all over Europe in the struggles of the Counter Reformation, but being an island, England came off lightly in these devastating affairs. Indeed the country benefited in many ways; Flemish and Walloon weavers fled to these shores to escape persecution.

Our developing mercantilism and industry was not held back. The realisation that a competent navy was essential for defence, and its subsequent strengthening, led to our own successful exploitation of the Americas, both in the forced diversion of Spanish treasure ships and the acquisition of a share of trade with the West Indies. In 1562 John Hawkins, who later re-organised the fleet before The Armada, made the first voyage of 'The Triangular Trade', - to Africa for slaves - deliver them to Hispaniola - sell them and return to England with the proceeds. The East India company was granted its charter by Elizabeth in 1600.

The forces of Islam, after finally completing the conquest of the Eastern Roman Empire with the fall of Constantinople in 1453, were at the gates of Vienna, but surprisingly enough, defeat in the East benefited us tremendously in the West. Many art and literary treasures from the Byzantine world were removed to Northern Italy, fuelling the Renaissance. Islamic Universities in Moorish Spain introduced the knowledge of the East to the Western world; just the indo-arabic numbering system, for example, caused a revolution in a multitude of arts and sciences. Without the idea of zero and having only the cumbersome Roman notation, even doing simple arithmetic, so necessary in the everyday transactions of a merchant, was an arduous task involving jettons on a chequer board.

Tudor coinage gives a measure of the change in the form of numbers. The gold crown of the rose issued in 1526 used the Arabic 8 in King Henry's title. Twenty five years later the beautiful new silver crown issued by Edward VI had the date 1551 in Arabic numerals. Although we still use roman numerals to date programmes on the television, (MMVI this year for 2006), this is more for ornament than utility. The modern world of space ships and nuclear energy could not exist without the use of arabic numerals, and it all began for us in the fifteenth and sixteenth centuries.

The economy improved by leaps and bounds despite decades of inflation. A Norfolk man, Thomas Gresham, built the first Royal Exchange and was knighted by Elizabeth for his pains. He also gave his name to the law that says 'Bad money drives out Good', a first step in providing a scientific basis for controlling the economy.

The succession to the crown was the abiding political problem of the sixteenth century. The end of the 30 year long Wars of the Roses in 1485 at Bosworth Field and the uniting of the Lancaster and York factions by the marriage of Henry Tudor to Elizabeth of York had produced a period of calm lasting till their second son, Henry VIII, failed to produce a son and heir with the ageing Catherine of Aragon, his first wife. He broke with Rome to obtain a divorce and began his series of disastrous marriages in the attempt to provide a clear successor to his crown.

One of the contenders for the English crown at the accession of Elizabeth I in 1558, (when Robert Greene was born), was Mary Stuart, Queen of the Scots. Mary was the granddaughter of Henry VII, (Queen Elizabeth II is of the fifteenth generation in the same line from Margaret, Queen of Scots, Henry VII's daughter), and had been brought up in France as a Catholic by her mother, Mary of Guise. Her husband, the Dauphin, was crowned Francis II of France in 1559, but on his death the following year Mary returned to Scotland and as a Catholic next in line to the throne of England became the source of plots and counterplots until her execution in 1587.

Elizabeth as a believer in the absolute power of the Monarchy, did not wish to be seen supporting Protestant rebels against their queen in Scotland but she had no alternative if she were to preserve her own country against its enemies. She was reluctantly the means of allowing John Knox to establish the Presbyterian church in Scotland. Elizabeth had throughout her 44 year reign, to make decisions that went against her principles. Not the least of these decisions was to sign the death warrant of her second cousin, Mary, Queen of Scots.

2   Elizabethan Drama

An Act of 1572 dealing with 'law and order' placed actors and minstrels, who were not in the employ of a nobleman of sufficient status, in the category of vagabonds and to be punished as such. The houses of the nobility usually had a room set aside for performances of various kinds and men were retained to provide the entertainment for their family and guests. This led to the formation of organised groups of players who, under the patronage of lords such as Dudley, the Earl of Leicester, were able to perform in public. The stage used by Leicester's players was in the courtyard of the Bull Inn, Bishopgate. Then James Burbage, manager of Leicester's men, opened the first purpose built theatre in Finsbury Fields in 1577. This he called, after the original Greek name for such a building, the 'Theatre'. A rival company opened the Curtain theatre nearby shortly afterwards. The great boom in stage plays in the last quarter of the century led to the building of the Rose (1588), the Swan (1595), the Globe (1599), and the Fortune (1600); all four theatres were in Southwark on the south bank of the River Thames outside the restrictions of the city authorities.

Throughout the period there was strong rivalry between the two principal theatre owners, Philip Henslowe and James Burbage. The same spirit of rivalry applied to their leading actors, James's son Richard and Edward Alleyn, who married Henslowe's stepdaughter Joan Woodward. Alleyn as Henslowe's son-in-law, became a partner in the theatre. At the age of twenty five Alleyn was actor manager of Lord Strange's men in 1591 at the Rose when performances of *Friar Bacon and Friar Bungay* are first recorded by Henslowe in his *Diary*.

Before the advent of public theatres, plays were acted mainly by amateurs, schoolchildren or village groups. The universities and schools acted comedy on classical lines both in Latin and English. The court supported the drama and Lyly's *Endimion* was written for and performed by the child actors of St. Paul's on New Year's Day before the Queen, at Greenwich in 1585. In it, the story of Cynthia's love for a mortal symbolises the queen's affection for Leicester. The public theatres, however, had to give their patrons something more to their taste and that, even more so than today, was violence. They had to compete with the delights of bear baiting and the ultimate theatrical horror of executions at Tyburn or Smithfield. At the same time the companies had to avoid anything that might appear to be a political statement against the crown or its supporters.

A great success, from its first production in 1587 and throughout the 1590's, was *Tamburlaine the Great*, written by Christopher Marlowe for Lord Strange's men, luridly recounting the exploits of Timur, the late 14th century cruel Asian conqueror of Persia, Russia and India. After capturing Delhi he slaughtered some 80,000 people and built pyramids of their skulls. The following year, in 1588, Thomas Kyd's *The Spanish Tragedy* joined Tamburlaine on the public stage proving a good second in its continuing popularity. In *The Spanish Tragedy* Kyd introduced a 'ghost' to encourage the revenge of a father for a murdered son. A year later in his version of *Hamlet* he dealt with the revenge of a son for a father involving a ghost, insanity, diabolic intrigue, physical horrors, much philosophising, and copious slaughter. Marlowe continued to lead the field in tragedy with *Doctor Faustus* where the theme was powerful intellect conquering nature by magic with tragical results.

This may have inspired Robert Greene to use the *Story of Friar Bacon and Friar Bungay* with its similar powerful scenes of magic also leading to conflict and loss of life, but mollified with romance and comedy. The authorship of *Arden of Feversham*, produced in 1590, has not been discovered but whoever was the author started the vogue for historical plays based on Hollinshed's Chronicles. *Arden* was unusual in that the play dealt with recent events, and did not involve lords and monarchs. Black Will and Shakebag carry out the murderous wishes of Alice, a veritable Lady Macbeth.

3   Robert Greene

Greene was born in Norwich in 1558 and probably attended the free grammar school, which at that time was situated at the Great Hospital. He went on to St. John's College, Cambridge where he received his BA in 1578, and MA in 1583 having migrated to Clare Hall.

(The young Princess Elizabeth was given a classical education by scholars from St. John's. She was not specifically trained for her job as queen since it was thought that she would never achieve that position. Such were her literary abilitities, encouraged by her tutors, that some scholars even think that Shakespeare's works were written by her).

Shortly after graduating as Bachelor of Arts, Greene travelled abroad, visiting France, Spain, Italy, Poland, Germany and Denmark. His scholarship was recognised by Oxford University where he was incorporated MA in 1588. On his return to England he married and had a child but when he had completed his course at Cambridge he left his family to pursue his writing in London. There he had a relationship with the sister of a ruffian called Cutting Ball who was hanged at Tyburn. His son by this liaison, called Fortunatus, survived his father by one year. According to one authority, Robert Greene produced some forty five independent publications before he died in 1592. These are the bare facts of his life but much more can be derived from various sources with varying degrees of certainty.

Much of his life story is derived from the book published posthumously in 1596, *A Groats-worth of Wit, bought with a Million of Repentance*, though it is hard to be sure what part is truth and what is fiction.

In it he relates how a rich merchant and usurer leaves to his eldest son Roberto, who is a scholar, a groat with which to make his fortune by using his wit. To his second son, Lucanio, he leaves his wealth which consisted of £30,000 cash, £15,000 in plate and jewels, £15,000 in bonds and specialities, and £900 per annum in land. The 'olde Groate' that he left to Lucanio's 'well red brother,' who is by the way married to a gentlewoman, '(being the stocke I first began with) wherewith I wish him to buy a groatsworth of wit'.

Elizabeth I, 1559-1560
Groat = four silver pennies

Greene recounts how he achieves Lucanio's downfall at the hands of Lamilia, a harlot of his acquaintance, who however refuses to share the proceeds of her cozening of Lucanio's fortune with him, Roberto. The latter's woes are overheard by a travelling player who engages him to write plays for his troupe.

Thus he makes his way but spends his gains on drink and women, ending up in the lowest dens of the criminal fraternity (who incidentally provide him with material for his Conny catching books). He ends up with the one groat left to him by his father, and says, "O now it is too late to buy witte with thee: and therefore will I see if I can sell to carelesse youth what I negligently forgot to buy". He then takes the part of Roberto "whose life in most parts agreeing with mine" and then as himself, Greene, says, "..though no man now be by, to doe me good, yet ere I die, I will by my repentance indeuor to doe all men good".

4   Publications

His first prose work was published in 1583 and he quickly became famous as a writer of romances. The style of his work was a development from the classical Latin and Greek authors, particularly in regard to his poems which were scattered throughout his prose. He and his contemporaries, Lyly, Nash and Marlowe, were known as 'The University Wits (or Pens)' because of their classical allusions and frequent use of the Latin language in their works.

They were all students at Cambridge and their knowledge of classical literature most probably came from the Royal Library that Sir Francis Walsingham was supposed to have left to the university, possibly part of the Parker library.

Sir Francis was Elizabeth's Secretary of State for seventeen years and her spy master. He had fifty three paid agents in foreign courts and correspondents supplying information in thirteen towns in France, seven in the Low Countries, five each in Italy and Spain, nine in Germany, three in the United Provinces and three in Turkey. He seems to have recruited at Cambridge where the parallels with the twentieth century spies Sir Anthony Blunt, Burgess and McLean are incredible. Christopher Marlowe was certainly one of his men and we may surmise that Greene too was involved.

Marlowe went up to Corpus Christi in 1580, graduated BA in 1584 and after an absence in France, returned to complete his MA by 1587 but only after a letter from the Privy Council excused his absence as 'it was in the service of the Queen'. Both Nashe and Greene were at St. John's during Marlowe's period at Cambridge and they must have been his comrades as they had the same interests. After taking his BA in 1580, Greene too travelled abroad, and on his return to complete his MA by 1583 he declared, "I light among wags as lewd as myself, with whom I consumed the flower of my youth." Was Robert Greene working for Walsingham in order to finance his continental adventures?

John Lyly, an Oxford graduate who also studied at Cambridge, was the first English writer of High Comedy and the two parts of his *Euphues* provided the style for Greene's *Euphues, His censure to Philautus* and his most successful novel, *Menaphon: Camilla's Alarum to Slumbering Euphues*, published in 1587/89. *Menaphon*, reprinted as *Greene's Arcadia* in later editions, contains some of his best poems including *Weepe not, my wanton, smile upon my knee*.

The unrestrained erotic nature of some of his poems, very much after the style of Ovid, reflects the hedonistic nature of Elizabethan society. When life could be cut short at any moment either by plague or violence, people who were able to, enjoyed their pleasures to the full. Robert Greene himself was a perfect example of this attitude to life.

Only one of Greene's poems, *A Maiden's Dream*, was published in its own right. It was composed: 'UPON THE DEATH OF THE RIGHT HONOURABLE SIR CHRISTOPHER HATTON, LATE LORD CHANCELLOR OF ENGLAND', in 1591, and a hint of patronage from certain gentry connected with Harleston can be read into the dedication to Elizabeth the wife of Sir William Newport, nephew and heir of Sir Christopher Hatton.

On the death of his uncle, Sir William Newport took the name Hatton. His wife Elizabeth was the daughter and heiress of Sir Francis Gawdy, Justice of the King's Bench, who was the youngest of three brothers. Their father was Thomas Gawdy who was the Duke of Norfolk's bailiff in his manor of Harleston and lived in what is now Reydon House on Redenhall Road where Francis was born in or about 1535. (Francis was baptised Thomas as were his two half brothers, but when it was obvious that they had survived to manhood he changed his name to Francis to avoid confusion.)

All three became eminent members of the legal profession. Francis married, in 1563 at Redenhall, Elizabeth, daughter and coheiress of Christopher Coningsby of Wallington, Norfolk. Elizabeth Gawdy, only child of Sir Francis was born at Wallington in 1571 and she married Sir William Newport who succeeded to the large property of his uncle Lord Chancellor Hatton in 1591.

> To the right worshipful, bountifull and vertuous
> Ladie, the Ladie Elizabeth Hatton, wife
> to the right Worshipful Sir William
> Hatton Knight, increase of
> all honorable vertues.

The Epistle Dedicatorie.

Mourning as well as many (right Worshipfull Ladie) for the late losse of the right Honorable your deceased Unckle, whose death being the common preiudice of the present age, was lamented of most (if not all) and I among the rest sorrowing

11

that my Countrie was depriued of him that liued not for himselfe, but for his Countrie, I began to call to mind what a subiect was ministred to the excellent wits of both Vniuersities to work vpon, when so worthie a Knight, and so vertuous a Iusticiarie, had by his death left many memorable actions performed in his life, deseruing highly by some rare pen to be registred. Passing ouer many daies in this muse, at last I perceiued mens humors slept, that loue of many friends followed no farther then their graues, that Art was growen idle, and either choice schollers feared to write of so high a subiect as his vertues, or else they dated their deuotions no farther then his life. While thus I debated with my selfe, I might see (to the great disgrace of the Poets of our time) some Mycanicall wits blow vp Mountaines, and bring forth mise, who with their follies did rather disparage his Honors, than decypher his vertues : beside, as *Virtutis comes est inuidia,* so base report who hath her tong blistered by slanderous enuie, began as farre as she durst, now after his death, to murmure, who in his life time durst not once mutter : wherupon touched with a zealous iealousie ouer his wonderfull vertues, I could not, whatsoeuer discredit I reapt by my presumption, although I did *Tenui Auena meditari,* but discouer the honorable qualities of so worthie a Counsellor, nor for anie priuat benefit I euer had of him, which should induce me fauorably to flatter his worthie partes, but onely that I shame to let slip with silence, the vertues and honors of so worthie a Knight, whose deserts had bin so many and so great towards al. Therfore (right worshipful Ladie) I drewe a fiction called A Maidens Dreame, which as it is *Enigmaticall,* so it is not without some speciall and considerate reasons.—Whose slender *Muse* I present vnto your Ladiship, induced therunto, first, that I know you are partaker of your husbands sorrowes for the death of his honourable Vncle, and desire to heare his honors put in memorie after his death, as you wished his aduancement in vertues to be great in his life : as also that I am your Ladiships poore Countriman, and haue long time desired to gratifie your right worshipfull father with some thing worthie him selfe. Which because I could not to my Content performe, I haue now taken oportunitie to shew my duetie to him in his daughter, although the gift be farre too meane for so worshipfull and vertuous a Lady. Yet hoping your Ladishippe will with courtesie fauour my presuming follies, and in gratious acceptance vouch of my well meant labours,

I humbly take my leaue.

Your Ladiships humbly at Commaund

R. GREENE. *Nordovicensis.*

It is said that Sir Francis owed his elevation to the bench to Queen Elizabeth's favoured chancellor Sir Christopher Hatton as, six months after it took place, his nephew married Francis's daughter. His next promotion, to the office of Lord Justice of the Common Pleas, probably resulted from the marriage of his grandchild and heiress Frances Hatton to Sir Robert Rich, afterwards second Earl of Warwick.

It would appear that Robert Greene in his dedication was referring to some previous association with Sir Francis Gawdy and hence perhaps with Harleston, the ancestral home of the Gawdy dynasty. He writes: "... as also that I am your ladyship's poor countryman, and have long time desired to gratify your right worshipful father with something worthy of himself. ....". He also confirms his Norwich origin by signing himself: R. Greene, *Nordivicensis*.

Judging by his works written when he thought he was dying, Greene was very religious and fearful of the after-life if he did not repent and receive forgiveness. He warned his fellow 'University Wits' of the retribution that they too would receive if they did not repent, particularly Marlowe for the atheistical beliefs that he put into the mouths of Faustus and Tamberlaine. It is no wonder that one of his contemporaries caricatured him seated quill pen in hand, writing at his table, wrapped in his shroud!

In his pamphlet, *A Quip for an Upstart Courtier*, Greene seems to identify himself with a poet, the last chosen of the twenty-four jurymen who were assembled to decide between 'velvet breeches' and 'cloth breeches', as to who had the right to call himself a true-born Englishman. The verdict of course was in favour of the Yeoman.

A

QVIP FOR AN VP-
start Courtier :

OR,

A quaint difpute between Veluet-
breeches and Cloth-breeches.

Wherein is plainely fet downe the diforders in all
Eftates and Trades.

LONDON

Imprinted by Iohn Wolfe, and are to bee fold at his
fhop at Poules chayne. 1592.

Five plays written by Greene have come down to us, all published posthumously. The first produced was probably *The Comical History of Alphonsus, King of Aragon* written in response to the enormous success of the tragedy, *Tamburlaine the Great*, composed by his friend, Christopher Marlowe. Alphonsus was no comparison to Tamburlaine, and Greene turned to comedy for success with *The Honourable History of Friar Bacon and Friar Bungay*.

Alphonsus has a link with the *Honourable History* as both of them have a scene involving a brazen head. The former's head represents Mahomet who speaks to the Turkish kings encouraging them to attack Alphonsus, but unlike Bacon's brazen head it does not destroy itself after speaking. (In Alphonsus, Greene refers to Mahomet as the God of the Turks). 'Old Mahomet's Head' was apparently in the props of The Admiral's Men, but may have been from Peele's play, '*Mahomet*'.

However, before writing *Friar Bacon and Friar Bungay*, he wrote *A Looking Glasse for London and England* in conjunction with Thomas Lodge. The *Looking Glasse* was an exposure of the vices prevalent in London of that day, and an earnest exhortation to amendment and repentance. What it especially denounces are luxury and lust, contempt of God, usury, the corruption of lawyers and judges, the debauchery of the lower classes, arrogance, the oppression of the poor, and ingratitude to parents. Greene compares London to Nineveh and predicts its destruction as a result if it doesn't repent of its sins, just as Nineveh was destroyed. Perhaps he composed this puritan drama with Lodge during one of his own brief periods of repentance.

Thomas Lodge was educated at Trinity College Oxford and studied law at Lincoln's Inn before taking up a literary career. Like Greene he followed Lyly's style with a euphuistic romance, *Rosalynde, Euphues Golden Legacie*. Shakespeare dramatised this work with little alteration in his *As You like It*.

Another play by Greene entered on the Stationers' Registers in 1594 was also said to have been a collaboration with Lodge though it may merely have had material added by him to the copy, published in 1598, which is the only one known. This was *The Scottish Historie of James IV, slaine at Flodden Field*, which also had a good run on the stage.

The Historie of Orlando Furioso One of the twelve pieres of France, 'As it was plaid before the Queenes Majesftie', published in London in 1594, is a very interesting composition of Greene's for several reasons. There exists in the collection at Dulwich College a manuscript copy of the script for the principal part of Orlando with interpolations in the handwriting of Edward Alleyn, who obviously played that part in the production which was recorded by his father-in-law, Philip Henslowe, in his diary for February 1591. It was written after 1588 as there is an allusion to the destruction of the Spanish Armada:

> 'And Spaniard tell, who, mand with mighty Fleetes,
> Came to subdue my Ilands to their King,
> Filling our Seas with stately Argosies,
> Caruels and Magars, hulkes of burden great;
> Which Brandemart rebated from his coast.'

It was very loosely based on an Italian poem by Ludovico Ariosto, *Orlando Furioso*, published in 1532.

Other prose works of his that were very popular were explanations of the methods used by the low life in London and the provinces to relieve unsuspecting victims of their property. This activity was termed '*Conny Catching*' and the reason for the name is well illustrated in the first page of one of these pamphlets, *The Art of Conny Catching*. Greene's knowledge of such criminal activities again illustrates perhaps the sort of company he kept and the life that he led.

He wrote a second part to *The Art of Conny Catching*, (it was obviously what we would call a 'best seller'), and intended to follow it with a complete *Blacke Booke* that would have named names and blown the gaff on the criminals involved in *Conny Catching* both in London and the provinces. He died before he could complete *The Blacke Book* and some scholar was persuaded to write *A Defence of Conny Catching*, signed by Cuthbert Conny-Catcher, 'Licentiate in Whittington Colledge'. Richard Whittington, of pantomime fame, left money for the rebuilding of Newgate prison after his death in 1423, and it is from this establishment that Cuthbert claims to have received his licentiate. Whittington College was the notorious Newgate Gaol.

THE ART OF CON-
ny-catching.

Here be requifit effectualy to act the Art of Cony-catching, thrée feueral parties: the Setter, the Verfer, and the Barnackle. The nature of the Setter, is to draw any perfon familiarly to drinke with him, which perfon they call

5   The *Friar Bacon and Friar Bungay* Play.

Robert Greene probably wrote *Friar Bacon and Friar Bungay* in 1590 as it was first recorded in Henslowe's diary as being performed in 1591/92. It is the first entry relating to theatrical performances in the diary and hence it was not necessarily the first performance ever. The actual entry reads as follows:

> In the name of God A men 1591
> beginge the 19 of febreary my
> lord stranges mene A ffoloweth
> 1591

Rd at fryer bacvne the 19 of febreary . . satterdaye . .xvij s iij d

it is also recorded for 25th March, 26th April, and the 6th May when Henslowe received, xv s vj d, xxiiij s, and xiiij s, respectively. The following year, 1592/3 (old date, where the year ended on 24th March), it was performed twice in January by Lord Strange's men and three times in January 1593/4 by the Earl of Sussex's men, according to the diary. From Easter 1593/4 the Queen's men and Lord Sussex's men together performed the play twice in April when xxxxiij s and xx s, was received. No further mention of *Friar Bacon and Friar Bungay* appears after June 15th of that year when the Lord Admiral's men and the Lord Chamberlain's men are the players recorded in the diary.

The basic story was taken from a prose work, the earliest extant copy of which, dated 1627, is entitled, *The Famous Historie of Fryer Bacon. Containing the wonderful things that he did in his Life: Also the manner of his Death; With the lives and Deaths of the two Conjurers, Bungye and Vandermast.*

This romance contains the same episodes as in the play where Bacon together with Bungay overcome the German magician, Vandermast in the presence of Henry III, and also where they create a Brazen Head that a devil will make speak, "by which hee would have walled England about with Brasse". In both versions the Friars fall asleep waiting for the head to speak leaving Bacon's comical assistant, Miles, to hear the few words "Time is", then "Time was", and finally "Time is past",

18

when the head collapses with a great commotion waking the Friars, who are cross with Miles for having wasted all their magical efforts.

However, in the prose romance Miles sings three songs to while away the waiting time. Considering Greene's poetic skills it is surprising that he does not include these in the play. Perhaps the words were not 'politically correct' for the public theatre of the time, or were lost before a version of the play was published in 1594. The third song, that was sung to the tune of *A Rich Merchant Man*, is worth quoting:

Time was when thou a kettle
Wert fill'd with better matter:
But Fryer Bacon did thee spoyle,
when he thy sides did batter.

Time was when Kings and Beggars
Of one poore stuffe had being:
Time waswhen office kept no knaves:
That time was worth seeing.

Time was when conscience dwelled
With men of occupattion:
Time was when Lawyers did not thrive
So well by mens vexation.

Time was a bowle of water
Did give the face reflection,
Time was when women knew no paint:
Which now they call complexion.

The romantic element in *Friar Bacon and Friar Bungay* is very like that in an anonymous, undated play, *A Pleasant Commodie of Faire Em The Millers Daughter of Manchester, with The Love of William the Conquerour*. Faire Em is the object of affection of a local gentleman, Manville, but two of William's Knights, Valingford and Mountney also desire her. They have stayed behind in England while William goes to Denmark to woo Blanche the king's daughter.

Scenes alternate between Denmark and Manchester as the plot unravels. William falls for his friend the Marquis of Lubeck's intended wife, Mariana, and thinks he has brought her to England in disguise to marry, but of course it is really Blanche. Em pretends she is deaf and blind in order to put off the two Knights, but that drives Manville to propose to Eliner a citizen of Chester's daughter. All ends happily however with William pairing with Blanche, Manville with Eliner, and Valingford with Faire Em.

The Manchester part of the plot of *Faire Em* must be based on a ballad licensed in 1580/1 entitled *The Miller's Daughter of Manchester* so it would not be necessary for the play's author to have personal knowledge of that locality, unlike Greene the author of *Friar*

Bacon and Friar Bungay whose knowledge of the Waveney Valley location of the romantic episodes in his play could only have been obtained from his own experience.

In *Friar Bacon and Friar Bungay*, Edward, Prince of Wales loves Margaret, the Fair Maid of Fressingfield. His friend Lacy, the Earl of Lincoln, disguised as a Beccles farmer, woos Margaret on the Prince's behalf at Harleston Fair. Two gentlemen, Lambert from Laxfield and Serlby the squire over her father's land, also seek her hand. Lacy falls for Margaret, tries to get Friar Bungay to marry them, but is frustrated by the Prince who employs Bacon's magical powers. Lambert and Serlby fight over her and kill each other, while their sons at Oxford seeing the quarrel through Bacon's magic glass, take sides and they stab each other.

Margaret threatens to enter a convent. Lacy offers his life to Edward who finally relents, and in a grand finale marries Eleanor of Castile, to whom he is betrothed and the Fair Maid of Fressingfield becomes the bride of Lacy, Earl of Lincoln. Places in Norfolk and Suffolk mentioned in this part of the play, not necessarily spelled correctly but more a phonetic interpretation by Greene, are as follows:

Harleston, Norfolk (on the Waveney, the border with Suffolk); Beccles, Suffolk (on the Waveney, the Norfolk border); Framlingham, Suffolk; Laxfield, Suffolk; Cratfield, Suffolk.

None of these places exists in any other known sixteenth century literary works. In addition Margaret's father is keeper of the deer park at Fressingfield where the Prince and his friends are hunting, disguised as mere gentlemen, where they meet the Fair Maid of Fressingfield in the opening scene.

The earliest printed version of 1594 very obviously differs from Greene's original manuscript. He would not have had the brazen head dashed to pieces before it says, "Time is past". Neither would he have neglected to write his Skeltonics in short lines as it is shown in the next section below. Unfortunately unless a manuscript copy of the play is unearthed, we will never know what Greene originally wrote.

6   The Influence of John Skelton

The poet John Skelton, who had been tutor to the young Duke of York, the future Henry VIII, was appointed rector of St. Mary's, Diss in or about 1504. He wrote most of his poems in Diss and one of them, *Ware The Hawk* which was aimed at a clergyman who apparently flew his hawk in St. Mary's, was obviously noticed by Greene. Skelton's works were published in London in 1568 well in time for Greene to copy his style, which became known as Skeltonics, in the speeches of Miles, Bacon's assistant:

Miles

And I with scientia.
And great diligentia,
Will conjure and charm,
To keep you from harm;
That utrum horum mavis,
Your very great navis,
Like Barclay's ship,
From Oxford do skip
With colleges and schools,
Full-loaden with fools.
Quid dicis ad hoc,
Worshipful Domine Dawcock?

Skelton in *Ware The Hawk*:

Whereto should I rehearse
The sentence of my verse?
In them be no schools
For brain-sick frantic fools.
Construas hoc,
Domine Dawcock!
Ware the hawk!

Miles here is referring to Alexander Barclay's *Ship of Fools* (1509) wherein fools of all kinds are shipped off to the Land of Fools. Greene uses, besides Skelton's style, his expression 'Domine Dawcock' from *Ware the Hawk* that translates as 'Master Fool'. 'Daw', literally Jackdaw but used here as a term for a fool, also occurs in the first part of Henry VI which Greene probably had a hand in writing,

"Good faith I am no wiser than a daw".

7   The Historical Setting of the Play

A reasonable guess perhaps for the time when the events in the play might have taken place would be mid-thirteenth century. King Henry III came to the throne in 1216 at the age of nine and declared that he had reached his majority and could assume his monarchical duties in 1226, marrying Eleanor of Provence ten years later, in 1236.

21

His son Edward was born in 1239 and Prince Edward's marriage to Eleanor of Castile, when he was just fifteen, gives a possible date, 1254, for the action of the play.

Edward, Prince of Wales: Marries Eleanor of Castile at the end of the play, (Historically 1254 when Eleanor was but a child). He boasts to Margaret in the scene where he is struggling with the jealousy of his friend Lacy and his duty to Eleanor, of being "at Damasco where he beat the Sarasens". He did not go on crusade until 1570 and was defeated by the Mameluks at Acre, never having been to Damascus. Henry III died while the prince was still abroad and he was acclaimed Edward I in his absence.

Emperor of Germany: Frederick II, King of the Romans and emperor elect never visited England and died in 1550. Henry III's brother, Richard of Cornwall, was elected King of the Romans in 1257, not a likely candidate for the character in the play.

Lacy, Earl of Lincoln: John de Lacy, constable of Chester and Lord of Clitheroe and Pontefract had married the countess of Winchester who resigned her claim to the Earldom of Lincoln to John de Lacy in the 1230's. This began the Lacy line of Earls that ended in 1348. Lacy was therefore an historical person.

Warren, Earl of Sussex: There was an Earl Warenne in the 13th century, who married Alesia de Lusignan in 1247. John de Warenne was however Earl of Surrey not Sussex. Although in 1305 he did style himself Earl of Sussex! The name Edward Warraine in the play's final scene is probably an error.

King of Castile: Alfonso, King of Castile and father of Eleanor the wife of Edward, Prince of Wales, never visited England.

Duke of Saxony: No historical record is found for such a person visiting England in the 13th century.

Eleanor of Castile: Edward's wife.

Vandermast: There is no historical record of such a person, but Greene uses the same name for a character in one of his books, *Greene's Vision*. A witty collection of licentious tales, written in the style of Chaucer's *Canterbury Tales*, was attributed to Greene who wrote the *Vision* in order to refute the allegation. The *Vision* is of Chaucer and John Gower, his poet friend, telling each other stories, Chaucer's supporting the writing of bawdy tales and Gower's the moral sort of works. The latter tells a tale of Alexander Vandermast of Antwerp being eaten up with a jealousy that his wife Theodora in no way deserves.

This leads to the possibility that Greene himself composed the prose work *The famous History of Fryer Bacon* and later rewrote it as a play in blank verse, *The Honorable Historie of frier Bacon, and frier Bongay*.

It would appear that *The Honourable History of Friar Bacon and Friar Bungay* was made up from a selection of stories about thirteenth century historical figures and events arranged, without any regard for chronology, around a continuous plot derived from a romantic verse drama involving aristocrats and commoners engaged in a love comedy complicated with disguises and cross affections. None of the other characters has any mention in historical records, except Bacon and Bungay who are dealt with in more detail below.

8   The Historical Friars, Bacon and Bungay

Bacon and Bungay were thirteenth century friars and did possibly meet as they both lived and worked in Oxford at various dates. Thomas Bungay was a divinity lecturer for the Franciscan order of which he was a member, at Oxford and Cambridge. He was vulgarly accounted a magician but, beyond that, little is known about him. On the other hand, Roger Bacon, also a friar of the order of St. Francis, besides having a similar reputation with the common man as a magician and creator of a speaking brass head, was the author of works that were much in advance of the time, on the subjects of Philosophy and Science. He proposed, what was then a dangerous heretical system of analysis, an appeal to experience in direct opposition to the scholastic method of argument from general premises based on authority.

Surprisingly enough his ideas were contained in treatises sent secretly to Pope Clement IV who, as papal legate in England before his elevation in 1265, had requested copies of Bacon's works. He was effectively the first English scientist and his experiments in the field of optics are said to have resulted in the invention of spectacles. The myth of his possession of a 'perspective glass', that allowed him to observe events occurring fifty miles away, probably arose from his suggestion of how a telescope might be constructed.

Some confusion existed among medieval chroniclers between Roger Bacon and Robert Bacon who was also a friar, but of the Dominican order, and who also taught at Oxford. In some reports it is Roger who confronted King Henry III at Oxford in 1233 with a sarcastic riddle: "Lord King, what is the greatest danger to those who are crossing the straits?" Henry replied in the words of Scripture that they could tell whose business was on the great deep. "Nay my lord", answered Bacon, "I will tell thee - Petrae et Rupes" - a bitter allusion to Peter des Roches, one of Henry's foreign favourites, who was bishop of Winchester. This tradition could have given rise to the idea of King Henry's meeting with Friar Bacon at Oxford which Greene used in the play.

9   Harleston Fair

The town had two fairs, the first was held on Midsummer Day, 24th June, the feast of the birth of St. John, the saint to whom the chapel of Harleston was dedicated. This was the fair at which Thomas might have bought fairings for Margaret in the play *The Honourable History of Friar Bacon and Friar Bungay* when she says to him:

> We country sluts of merry Fresingfield
> Come to buy needless noughts to make us fine,
> And look that yong-men should be francke this day,
> And court vs with such fairings as they can.
> Phoebus is blythe and frolicke looks from heauen
> As when he courted louely Semele,
> Swearing the pedles shall haue emptie packs,
> If that faire wether may make chapmen buy

In the time of Henry III, when the play was set, the chapmen and Thomas would have needed that king's hammered silver pennies to buy their goods and fairings.

Henry III, 1216-1272

Short Cross Penny

A second fair was granted by Henry III to Roger le Bygod, Earl of Norfolk and Marshal of England, to last eight days, namely the vigil and day of decollation of St. John the Baptist, and six days after. The feast day of the saint's beheading was August 29th.

10   Elizabethan Harleston

Harleston was and still is in the parish of Redenhall and the rector from 1597-1629, Richard More, reported 600 communicants in the parish. The population of Redenhall, Harleston and Wortwell would have been therefore about 2,500, mainly living in Harleston at the end of Elizabeth's reign. Harleston's weekly market, held on a Wednesday, was the most important for miles around and had existed from time immemorial. It was the reason for the existence of the town and provided occupation for the inhabitants. Trades associated with the droving of cattle, such as tanners and leather workers, were important.

Provision of fare and accommodation for travellers was another source of work; Harleston was on the main route from Yarmouth to London. The Swan Inn was thought to have been built by Robert Cook, who in 1551 obtained a pardon under the Great Seal for all treasons etc. He had probably been involved in Kett's rebellion, two years previously. The coins in circulation at that time, easing the wheels of commerce in Harleston, would have been silver shillings and sixpences of Edward VI, Philip and Mary, and Elizabeth:

Edward VI 1547-53
Hammered Silver Shilling,
minted in 1551

Philip and Mary, 1554-58
Hammered Sixpence

Elizabeth I, 1558-1603
Hammered Sixpence

Harleston market and fair in medieval times would have been held in the triangle bounded by the roads now called: Broad Street, Old Market Place, Exchange Street, and The Thoroughfare. Within this area there would have been the Old Chapel where the present HSBC Bank is situated and next to it would have been the Market Toll house and an Inn with brewery attached. The rest of the area would have been filled with market stalls and butchers' shambles, arranged in rows with narrow passages between. The whole would have been supervised by the Lord of the Manor's Bailiff.

In Tudor times the transfer of wealth from the church to the laity created an economic boom that in Harleston resulted in the development of permanent stalls, shops and other buildings in the medieval Market Place. The passages now running transversely, East/West across the area, parallel to the present Union Street, (formerly known as Cross Street), are a palimpsest of the original rows between the market stalls. In addition many of the medieval houses, usually gable end to the market area, were 'modernised' inside and refronted in Tudor Style.

The richer occupants had pleasure gardens constructed behind their properties and the industries associated with building, woodworking, cattle, horses, textiles and beer were developed behind the inns. The medieval drink was ale, but the introduction of hops from the Low Countries had produced a drink with keeping qualities, beer, and from that time on England became a nation of beer drinkers.

11   Harleston Fair and The Ridolfi Plot

A crucial question in determining the origin of the sub-plot in *The Honourable History of Friar Bacon and Friar Bungay*, is what brought the Harleston area to the attention of Robert Greene? One event that would have been very much talked about in Greene's home town, Norwich, when he was twelve years of age, was the rebellion that having started in Norwich, was planned to involve a general rising at Harleston Fair on 24th June 1570.

The defeat of Mary, Queen of Scots by her rebellious Scottish lords at Langside in 1568, and her consequent flight to England, started a sequence of events that led eventually to her execution eighteen years later. The problem that Mary's presence posed for Elizabeth was that since she had not married and produced an heir to retain the supremacy of the crown both spiritual and secular, her half-sister Mary, who was her natural successor, as an ardent Catholic was likely to overturn all the advances in national government that the English Reformation had brought about and return the nation once more to the control of the Pope in Rome. This transformation would not necessarily occur without bloodshed and Mary's supporters were very likely to accelerate the process by disposing of Elizabeth.

The Pope, and his supporter Philip II of Spain, saw their opportunity to re-conquer the soul of England by supporting Mary and her followers. Philip's ambassador, De Spesa, sought to make contact with and to act as an intermediary between disaffected persons and his Catholic masters in a zealous attempt at counter-reformation. He was naturally well watched by Walsingham but achieved a great deal through the services of a Florentine banker, Ridolfi, who in his normal course of business could pass on messages and financial support from the Pope and Spain. He was himself a born plotter and set up a whole network of people who became involved in his grand design to rid England of its Protestant queen and bring it back under the thumb of the Pope. Thomas Howard, fourth Duke of Norfolk, was one of his targets. Howard had been persuaded that by marrying Mary, Queen of Scots, he would benefit the country and himself at the same time. In the event of Mary being restored to the Scottish throne he would become King Consort and stepfather of her son James who would succeed to the English crown.

Even better, if she supplanted Elizabeth, he would become King Consort of England. This would in his eyes sort out the problems of the English succession that had been bedevilling the reign of our virgin queen. Elizabeth, however, was far from pleased with the idea. Her favourite, Dudley, Earl of Leicester, seemed to support Norfolk, since the field would be open for him then to fulfil his dream and marry Elizabeth.

The Northern Earls, Northumberland and Westmorland, having been primed by Ridolfi with twelve thousand papal crowns, were ready to start the rebellion, but Norfolk lost his nerve and retired to his palace at Kenninghall. Elizabeth was furious and sent for him to explain himself but when he did return under escort to London, he was diverted to imprisonment at the Tower.

The Earls, including Westmorland, egged on by his wife who was Norfolk's sister, nonetheless raised the standard of Holy war and marched South. Having reached Selby, within striking distance of Tutbury where they had hoped to release Mary, they were frustrated by her gaolers having removed her to Coventry. On the 25th November 1569 they began their retreat North, and when no help arrived from Alva in the Spanish Netherlands, the Earls having captured Hartlepool as a suitable port for his troops to disembark, they fled into Scotland and eventually to exile in the Netherlands.

Meanwhile, the Duke's friends in East Anglia should have risen in support, but with their leader held in the Tower nothing much happened. A few Kenninghall men, tenants of the Duke must have heard that the North had risen and on the 6th of December they tried to raise forces on their own initiative, but with no direction this action quickly died. The Justices, including Thomas Gawdy, serjeant at law, sentenced the chief conspirators to prison to await Her Majesty's pleasure.

The following year revolt did break out in Norwich. The leader was John Appleyard whose half sister, Amy Robsart, was Robert Dudley's ill fated wife. Their cry was 'Out with the Strangers', (the Flemings and Walloons who had been encouraged by the Queen to escape persecution in their native country and revive the textile trades in London and Norwich with their New Draperies).

The intention was to play on the anti-foreigner feelings of the common people but the real aims, as revealed subsequently, were to raise sufficient forces locally so that together with other contingents from the Norfolk/Suffolk borders they would take Norwich for the Catholic cause, and then join up with Alva's troops, whom they expected to land at Yarmouth, from The Low Countries . Together they would march on London, depose the Queen and restore the old faith in England.

The rallying point for the main rising was to be at Harleston Fair which was held on 24th June, the feast of St. John the Baptist. The chapel of St. John had been dissolved under Edward VI but the annual fair continued to attract people from far and wide and seemed to Appleyard and his advisors an ideal place for their purpose. They may have been influenced by Brian Holland who had joined their councils on 6th June, as Holland was from the parish of Redenhall that contained Harleston. He had been appointed escheator of Norfolk by the Duke in 1556/7 and the Holland family administered much of the Duke of Norfolk's property in Norfolk and Suffolk.

Before the Fair the authorities had been tipped off and the rebels were rounded up and confined in Norwich prison. One who managed to escape was a servant of the Duke of Norfolk who, significantly, was sent over to France by the Bishop of Ross. John Leslie, Bishop of Ross, saw himself as the leader of the counter Reformation in Scotland. It was he who had been commissioned by the Catholic lords on the death of Francis II of France, Mary's husband, to invite her back to Scotland. He became indispensable to Mary as her confidential secretary and was deeply implicated in all attempts, especially those involving Roberto Ridolfi, to liberate her from captivity in England.

However, the Northern rebellion, the Kenninghall fiasco and the Harleston Fair rising, without the central figure of the Duke of Norfolk had all failed miserably. The Northern Counties had been laid waste, seven hundred and fifty rebels executed, and the remainder deprived of their ancient leaders. East Anglia had been subdued and as an example to others Throgmorton, Brooke and Redman had been hanged, drawn and quartered at the gates of Norwich Castle.

John Throgmorton, on the gallows, confessed that he was the arch conspirator, but in 1571 his widow Margaret was granted certain of his property including land in Suffolk which he had jointly owned with Thomas Gawdy. Robert Greene could hardly have missed all this excitement on his own doorstep. He may have pushed his way to the front of the crowds enjoying the ghoulish spectacle at the castle gates.

The trial judges led by Thomas, Lord Wentworth, the Lord Lieutenant of the county, were: the Chief Justice of the Queen's Bench, the Attorney General, the Solicitor General, the principal Justices of the Peace in the county (including Thomas Gawdy). The Chief Justice and his retinue must have arrived at Norwich in some style and no doubt young Robert would have watched their arrival at their lodgings at the Crown Inn, Elm Hill, which was not far from his probable home in Tombland.

Although all the above events were obviously engineered by Ridolfi, the next conspiracy in which he was involved as central character was given the particular name 'Ridolfi Plot' by historians because it was so well documented and easily identified as a single coherent attempt to subvert the government of England. Having learnt from the previous attempts, Walsingham made sure that every effort was made to intercept and decode all correspondence between Mary, Queen of Scots, the Bishop of Ross, Philip II, the Pope, De Stresa, the Duke of Norfolk and anyone else who might be involved. As a result all was discovered, the conspirators arrested and interrogated, and the Duke tried, found guilty of treason, and executed.

12   Robert Greene and William Shakespeare

There is very little evidence to connect William Shakespeare the author of the plays published in 1623 in The First Folio with the man of the same name born in 1564 in Stratford on Avon, dying there in 1616. To bring the latter on to the theatrical scene in London before his name appears as an actor in the accounts for a performance at Court at Christmas 1594 with the Chamberlain's men, scholars through the years have relied entirely on the mention of a 'Shake-scene' in Greene's *Groatsworth of Wit*. The relevant extract is quoted overleaf.

To thofe Gentlemen his Quondam acquaintance,
that fpend their wits in making plaies, R.G.
wifheth a better exercife,and wifdome
to preuent his extremities.

IF wofull experience may moue you (Gentlemen)to
beware, or vnheard of wretchednes intreate you to
take heed : I doubt not but you wil looke backe with
forrow on your time paft, and indeuour with repentance to fpend that which is to come. Wonder not, (for
with thee wil I firft begin)thou famous gracer of Tragedians, that Greene, who hath faid with thee(like the
foole in his heart)Thereis no God, fhould now giue
glorie vnto his greatnes : for penetrating is his power,
his hand lyes heauie vpon me, hee hath fpoken vnto mee
with a voice of thunder, and I haue felt he is a God that
can punifh enemies. Why fhould thy excellent wit, his
gift, bee fo blinded, that thou fhouldft giue no glorie to
the giuer? Is it peftilent Machiuilian pollicy that thou
haft ftudied ? O peeuifh follie ! What are his rules but
meere confufed mockeries, able to extirpate in fmall
time the generation of mankind . For if Sic volo, fic iu-
beo, hold in thofe that are able to commaund : and if it
be lawfull Fas & nefas to do any thing that is benefici-
all ; onely Tyrants fhould poffeffe the earth, and they
ftriuing to exceed in tyrannie, fhould each to other be a
flaughter man ; till the mightieft outliuing all, one
ftroke were lefte for Death, that in one age mans life
fhould end. The brocher of this Diabolicall Atheifme
is dead, and in his life had neuer the felicitie hee aymed
at : but as he began in craft; liued in feare, and ended in
defpaire. Quàm infcrutabilia funt Dei iudicia ? This
murderer of many brethren, had his confcience feared
like Caine : this betrayer of him that gaue his life for
him, inherited the portion of Iudas : this Apoftata peri-
fhed as ill as Iulian : and wilt thou my friend be his dif-
ciple ? Looke but to me, by him perfwaded to that libertie, and thou fhalt find it an infernall bondage. I knowe
the leaft of my demerits merit this miferable death, but
wilfull ftriuing againft knowne truth, exceedeth all the
terrors of my foule . Defer not(with me)till this laft
point of extremitie; for litle knowft thou how in the end
thou fhalt be vifited.
    With thee I ioyne yong Iuuenall, that byting Sa-
tyrift, that laftly with mee together writ a Comedie.

31

Sweet boy, might I aduise thee, be aduisde, and get not
many enemies by bitter wordes : inueigh against vaine
men, for thou canst do it, no man better, no man so well :
thou hast a libertie to reprooue all, and name none ; for
one being spoken to, all are offended; none being blamed
no man is iniured. Stop shallow water still running, it
will rage, or tread on a worme and it will turne : then
blame not Schollers vexed with sharpe lines, if they re-
proue thy too much liberty of reproofe.

And thou no lesse deseruing than the other two, in
some things rarer, in nothing inferiour ; driuen (as my
selfe) to extreme shifts, a little haue I to say to thee: and
were it not an idolatrous oth, I would sweare by sweet
S. George, thou art vnworthy better hap, sith thou dependest on so meane a stay. Base minded men all three
of you, if by my miserie you be not warnd: for vnto none
of you (like mee) sought those burres to cleaue : those
Puppets (I meane) that spake from our mouths, those
Anticks garnisht in our colours. Is it not strange, that
I, to whom they all haue beene beholding: is it not like
that you, to whome they all haue beene beholding, shall
(were yee in that case as I am now) bee both at once of
them forsaken ? Yes trust them not : for there is an vp-
start Crow, beautified with our feathers, that with his
Tygers hart wrapt in a Players hyde, supposes he is as
well able to bombast out a blanke verse as the best of
you : and beeing an absolute Iohannes fac totum, is in
his owne conceit the onely Shake-scene in a countrey.
O that I might intreat your rare wits to be imploied in
more profitable courses : & let those Apes imitate your
past excellence, and neuer more acquaint them with
your admired inuentions. I knowe the best husband of
you all will neuer proue an Vsurer, and the kindest of
them all will neuer proue a kind nurse : yet whilest you
may, seeke you better Maisters ; for it is pittie men of
such rare wits, should be subiect to the pleasure of such
rude groomes.

In this I might insert two more, that both haue
writ against these buckram Gentlemen : but lette their
owne workes serue to witnesse against their owne wic-
kednesse, if they perseuere to maintaine any more such
peasants. For other new-commers, I leaue them to the
mercie of these painted monsters, who (I doubt not)
will driue the best minded to despise them : for the rest,
it skils not though they make a ieast at them.

32

But now returne I againe to you three, knowing my miſerie is to you no newes : and let mee hartily in-treat you to be warned by my harms. Delight not (as I haue done) in irreligious oathes ; for from the blaſphe-mers houſe, a curſe ſhall not depart. Deſpiſe drunken-nes, which waſteth the wit, and maketh men all equall vnto beaſts. Flie luſt, as the deathſman of the ſoule, and defile not the Temple of the holy Ghoſt. Abhorre thoſe Epicures, whoſe looſe life hath made religion lothſome to your eares : and when they ſooth you with tearms of Maiſterſhip, remember Robert Greene, whome they haue often ſo flattered, periſhes now for want of com-fort. Remember Gentlemen, your liues are like ſo ma-ny lighted Tapers, that are with care deliuered to all of you to maintaine : theſe with wind-puft wrath may be extinguiſht, which drunkennes put out, which negli-gence let fall : for mans time is not of it ſelfe ſo ſhort, but it is more ſhortned by ſinne. The fire of my light is now at the laſt ſnuffe, and for want of wherewith to ſu-ſtaine it, there is no ſubſtance lefte for life to feede on. Truſt not then (I beſeech ye) to ſuch weake ſtaies : for they are as changeable in minde, as in many attyres. Wel, my hand is tyrde, and I am forſt to leaue where I would begin : for a whole booke cannot containe their wrongs, which I am forſt to knit vp in ſome fewe lines of words.

Deſirous that you ſhould liue, though himſelfe be dying:
Robert Greene.

Now to all men I bid farewel in like ſort, with this conceited Fable of that olde Comedian Aeſope.

Since *Groatsworth* was written on Greene's death bed, the date must be 1592. On this passage is built the evidence for the authorship by Shakespeare of a number of plays, particularly, the three parts of Henry VI. It has been shown that a more likely candidate for the Shake-scene was Edward Alleyn, the actor manager with Henslowe at the Rose Theatre. He was a great tragedian who could turn his hand to writing and probably helped to finish the script for *Henry VI Part One* which had been written in a great hurry ready for the opening of the rebuilt Rose, and incorporated dramatic elements using a new feature on the Rose, the turret, that Alleyn wanted to exploit.

33

In the event, *Henry VI Part One*, which had been a collaboration between Peele, Greene and Marlowe as well as Alleyn, was a great success for Henslowe and his son-in-law Edward Alleyn.

The plays *Henry VI Parts Two & Three* in the First Folio were developments by Shakespeare of, *The First Part of the Contention of the Two Famous Houses of York and Lancaster* and *The True Tragedy of Richard Duke of York*, two plays ascribed to Marlowe. Hence the often quoted, "an upstart Crow beautified with our feathers, that with his Tygers hart wrapt in a Players hyde!", in the *Groatsworth of Wit* parodies, "Oh Tygers hart wrapt in a womans hide" in the original version of *Henry VI Part Three*, written by Marlowe, not Shakespeare who only modified it for his version published in 1623.

Greene in his *Groatsworth of Wit* admonishes his fellow dramatists, "Thou famous gracer of Tragedians", (Christopher Marlowe), ".... young Juvenal, that biting satirist, that lastly with me wrote a comedy, (Thomas Nashe), "And thou no less deserving than the other two ..... I would swear by sweet St. George, thou art unworthy better hap, sith thou dependest on so meane a stay", (George Peele), where he launches into an attack on the players who have used his and their words, to feed their stomachs while he lies starving, has the reference to Shake-scene that Shakespeare scholars take as the first mention of the Bard of Avon. "... is it not like that you, to whom they all have been beholding ......: Yes trust them not: for there is an upstart Crow, beautified with our feathers, that with his *Tygers hart wrapt in a Players hyde*, supposes he is as well able to bombast out a blanke verse as the best of you: and being an absolute *Johanes factotum*, is in his own conceit the only Shake-scene in a countrey".

The appellation Shake-scene is quite clearly a reference to an actor who bombasted out in blank verse the parts of great men such as Tamburlaine and the Duke of York in *The True Tragedy of Richard Duke of York*, that appeared 23 years later in Shakespeare's revision *Henry VI Part Three*. The whole passage is bewailing the fact that an actor manager, who can also put his hand to writing, makes a fortune out of the works of Greene, Marlowe, Peele, and Nashe. Who else could this be but Edward Alleyn; the man who made enough money from the theatre to found the college at Dulwich which commemorates his name?

A

PLEASANT

Conceited Comedie

CALLED,

Loues labors loſt.

As it vvas preſented before her Highnes
this laſt Chriſtmas.

Newly corrected and augmented
By W. Shakeſpere.

Imprinted at London by W. W.
for *Cutbert Burby.*
1598.

Evidence for Shakespeare writing plays in London before 1592 comes from publications such as the above title page for the play *Loves Labours Lost* as it was played before Queen Elizabeth 'this last Christmas'. Since it was published in 1598 and 'Newly corrected and augmented by W. Shakespere', it would seem that previous versions by an unknown author had existed before this date, possibly before Greene's *Groatsworth of Wit* was written in 1592, and corrected and added to by William Shakespeare. Not very convincing evidence in favour of Greene accusing Shakespeare of taking advantage of him and his associates before 1592!

13 Summary

It is likely that Robert Greene was born in the Tombland area of Norwich in 1558. His father was probably a tradesman who was sufficiently well off to be able to send him to St. John's College, Cambridge.

His fictional work *A Groatsworth of Wit* supposedly represents him as being the eldest son of a merchant who has made a considerable fortune by lending money at a high rate of interest. The merchant on his death bed leaves his business and his fortune to Robert's brother, and only a fourpenny piece for Robert with which to make his living, by buying wit (or education) with it. This is obviously a highly coloured view of what really happened. More likely his father was only able to scrape enough money together to send one son to Cambridge while the other stayed at home and took up his father's trade that was, by elimination from the sixteenth century Norwich Church registers, probably that of a saddler. Greene was a sizar at St. John's which means he had to help pay for his course by doing work for the richer undergraduates. He must have got hold of enough money to pay for his travels on the continent, and this may be what he calls a Groats worth of Wit, or perhaps it was his inheritance that he managed to persuade his father to part with.

He made contact with like minded fellows at Cambridge where they had access to a library of classical and modern printed works and manuscripts. This library was perhaps the one donated by Archbishop Parker who was the patron of Christopher Marlowe, one of Greene's fellow writers, although one source suggests that Francis Walsingham, the Queen's Secretary of State, had given his library to the university. Wherever they got their inspiration from, the so-called 'university wits', Greene, Marlowe, and Nashe began their literary careers while still at Cambridge. Greene with prose romances containing numerous poems and only later following Marlowe with dramatic works.

Nashe, the youngest of the three, also started with mainly satirical prose works. He seemed to be a particular friend of Greene. His first work, published in 1589, was a vitriolic review of current literature that he prefixed to Greene's *Menaphon*. The latter's illness and death was attributed to a surfeit of Rhenish wine and pickled herrings taken at supper with Thomas Nashe.

Greene's romances were very popular when they were written but have not survived the test of time. Certainly his dramatic works although still having some interest to students of Elizabethan drama do not compare with those of his successor Shakespeare as published in the 'First Folio' (1623). But by concentrating on Greene's mention of a 'Shake-scene' in his *Groatsworth of Wit* as the only evidence for Shakespeare to have been active in London four years before the publication of his first works, historians of the drama have neglected the importance of Greene as a dramatist in his own right and as an essential precursor for the development of those incomparable plays in the 'First Folio'.

'Shake-scene' may or may not have referred to Shakespeare but Greene definitely used a real location in his home county of Norfolk for the meeting of the principal lovers, Lacy, Earl of Lincoln and the 'Fair Maid of Fressingfield, in his most successful play, *The Honorable Historie of Frier Bacon and Frier Bungay*. Harleston in the Waveney Valley certainly does exist and is proud to have been included in this play; one of the earliest dramatic works of the English Renaissance; even though Harleston Fair may have come into the ken of Robert Greene as the proposed start of the English Counter Reformation in 1570. He did, of course, know Francis Gawdy who was born in Reydon House, Harleston.